MOUNTAIN MOVING

2026 PLANNER

This Planner Belongs to

Name : _____

Date : _____

Address : _____

_____

_____

A Gift From : _____

2026 Holidays

United States	The Bahamas
1/1 New Year's Day	1/1 New Year's Day
1/19 Martin Luther King Jr. Day	10/1 Majority Rule Day
2/16 Presidents' Day	12/1 Majority Rule Day (observed)
5/25 Memorial Day	3/4 Good Friday
6/19 Juneteenth	6/4 Easter Monday
7/3 Independence Day (observed)	25/5 Whit Monday
7/4 Independence Day	5/6 Randol Fawkes Labour Day
9/7 Labor Day	10/7 Independence Day
10/12 Columbus Day	3/8 Emancipation Day
11/11 Veterans Day	12/10 National Heroes Day
11/26 Thanksgiving Day	25/12 Christmas Day
12/25 Christmas Day	26/12 Boxing Day

2026

JANUARY

S	M	T	W	T	F	S
				1	2	3
4	5	6	7	8	9	10
11	12	13	14	15	16	17
18	19	20	21	22	23	24
25	26	27	28	29	30	31

FEBRUARY

S	M	T	W	T	F	S
1	2	3	4	5	6	7
8	9	10	11	12	13	14
15	16	17	18	19	20	21
22	23	24	25	26	27	28

MARCH

S	M	T	W	T	F	S
1	2	3	4	5	6	7
8	9	10	11	12	13	14
15	16	17	18	19	20	21
22	23	24	25	26	27	28
29	30	31				

APRIL

S	M	T	W	T	F	S
			1	2	3	4
5	6	7	8	9	10	11
12	13	14	15	16	17	18
19	20	21	22	23	24	25
26	27	28	29	30		

MAY

S	M	T	W	T	F	S
					1	2
3	4	5	6	7	8	9
10	11	12	13	14	15	16
17	18	19	20	21	22	23
24	25	26	27	28	29	30
31						

JUNE

S	M	T	W	T	F	S
	1	2	3	4	5	6
7	8	9	10	11	12	13
14	15	16	17	18	19	20
21	22	23	24	25	26	27
28	29	30				

JULY

S	M	T	W	T	F	S
			1	2	3	4
5	6	7	8	9	10	11
12	13	14	15	16	17	18
19	20	21	22	23	24	25
26	27	28	29	30	31	

AUGUST

S	M	T	W	T	F	S
						1
2	3	4	5	6	7	8
9	10	11	12	13	14	15
16	17	18	19	20	21	22
23	24	25	26	27	28	29
30	31					

SEPTEMBER

S	M	T	W	T	F	S
		1	2	3	4	5
6	7	8	9	10	11	12
13	14	15	16	17	18	19
20	21	22	23	24	25	26
27	28	29	30			

OCTOBER

S	M	T	W	T	F	S
				1	2	3
4	5	6	7	8	9	10
11	12	13	14	15	16	17
18	19	20	21	22	23	24
25	26	27	28	29	30	31

NOVEMBER

S	M	T	W	T	F	S
1	2	3	4	5	6	7
8	9	10	11	12	13	14
15	16	17	18	19	20	21
22	23	24	25	26	27	28
29	30					

DECEMBER

S	M	T	W	T	F	S
		1	2	3	4	5
6	7	8	9	10	11	12
13	14	15	16	17	18	19
20	21	22	23	24	25	26
27	28	29	30	31		

Be encouraged to have Mountain Moving *Faith* in 2026!

"By Faith" From Hebrews 11:1, 4, 5, 7a, 8, 11-12, 20-23, 30-31

1 Now faith is the substance of things hoped for, the evidence of things not seen.

4 By faith Abel offered to God a more excellent sacrifice than Cain, through which he obtained witness that he was righteous, God testifying of his gifts; and through it he being dead still speaks.

5 By faith Enoch was taken away so that he did not see death, "and was not found, because God had taken him;" for before he was taken he had this testimony, that he pleased God.

7 By faith Noah, being divinely warned of things not yet seen, moved with godly fear, prepared an ark for the saving of his household.

8 By faith Abraham obeyed when he was called to go out to the place which he would receive as an inheritance. And he went out, not knowing where he was going.

11 By faith Sarah herself also received strength to conceive seed, and she bore a child when she was past the age, because she judged Him faithful who had promised. 12 Therefore from one man, and him as good as dead, were born as many as the stars of the sky in multitude—innumerable as the sand which is by the seashore.

20 By faith Isaac blessed Jacob and Esau concerning things to come.

21 By faith Jacob, when he was dying, blessed each of the sons of Joseph, and worshiped, leaning on the top of his staff.

22 By faith Joseph, when he was dying, made mention of the departure of the children of Israel, and gave instructions concerning his bones.

23 By faith Moses, when he was born, was hidden three months by his parents, because they saw he was a beautiful child; and they were not afraid of the king's command.

30 By faith the walls of Jericho fell down after they were encircled for seven days.

31 By faith the harlot Rahab did not perish with those who did not believe, when she had received the spies with peace.

JANUARY

MOUNTAIN MOVING

Faith

Sets a Firm Foundation

Now faith is the substance of things hoped for, the
evidence of things not seen.
- Hebrews 11:1

Overview

sun	mon	tue	wed	thu	fri	sat
				1 New Year's Day (US & BS)	2	3
4	5	6	7	8	9	10 Majority Rule Day
11	12 Majority Rule Day Observed	13	14	15	16	17
18	19 Martin Luther King Jr Day	20	21	22	23	24
25	26	27	28	29	30	31

"Mountain Moving *Faith*" Note

Special Days

Week in View

dates: Thursday, January 1 to Sunday, January 4

Thursday	**Friday**	**Weekend**

Faith verse for the week:

By faith we understand that the worlds were framed by the word of God, so that the things which are seen were not made of things which are visible.
Hebrews 11:3

Action Plan
for the Week

MOUNTAIN MOVING *Faith* FOCUS
FOR THIS WEEK!

....

....

....

THIS WEEK'S GOALS

✐ ....

✐ ....

✐ ....

PRIORITIES

✐ ....

✐ ....

✐ ....

✐ ....

PRAYER CONCERNS

✐ ....

✐ ....

✐ ....

✐ ....

GIVE THANKS FOR

✐ ....

✐ ....

✐ ....

✐ ....

Week in View

Monday	Tuesday	Wednesday

Thursday	Friday	Weekend

Faith verse for the week:

For in it the righteousness of God is revealed from faith to faith; as it is written, "The just shall live by faith."
Romans 1:17

Action Plan
for the Week

MOUNTAIN MOVING *Faith* FOCUS
FOR THIS WEEK!

....

....

....

THIS WEEK'S GOALS

◦ ....

◦ ....

◦ ....

PRIORITIES

◦ ....

◦ ....

◦ ....

◦ ....

PRAYER CONCERNS

◦ ....

◦ ....

◦ ....

◦ ....

GIVE THANKS FOR

◦ ....

◦ ....

◦ ....

◦ ....

Week in View

Monday	Tuesday	Wednesday

Thursday	Friday	Weekend

Faith verse for the week:

For we walk by faith, not by sight.
2 Corinthians 5:7

Action Plan
for the Week

MOUNTAIN MOVING *Faith* FOCUS
FOR THIS WEEK!

....

....

....

THIS WEEK'S GOALS

✺ ....

✺ ....

✺ ....

PRIORITIES

✺ ....

✺ ....

✺ ....

✺ ....

PRAYER CONCERNS

✺ ....

✺ ....

✺ ....

✺ ....

GIVE THANKS FOR

✺ ....

✺ ....

✺ ....

✺ ....

✺ ....

Week in View

dates: Monday, January 19 to Sunday, January 25

Monday	Tuesday	Wednesday

Thursday	Friday	Weekend

Faith verse for the week:

For by grace you have been saved through faith, and
that not of yourselves; it is the gift of God.
Ephesians 2:8

Action Plan
for the Week

MOUNTAIN MOVING *Faith* FOCUS
FOR THIS WEEK!

....

....

....

THIS WEEK'S GOALS

✠ ....

✠ ....

✠ ....

PRIORITIES

✠ ....

✠ ....

✠ ....

✠ ....

PRAYER CONCERNS

✠ ....

✠ ....

✠ ....

✠ ....

GIVE THANKS FOR

✠ ....

✠ ....

✠ ....

✠ ....

✠ ....

Week in View

dates: **Monday, January 26** to **Sunday, February 1**

Monday	Tuesday	Wednesday

Thursday	Friday	Weekend

Faith verse for the week:

But without faith it is impossible to please Him, for he who comes to God must believe that He is, and that He is a rewarder of those who diligently seek Him.

Hebrews 11:6

Action Plan
for the Week

MOUNTAIN MOVING *Faith* FOCUS
FOR THIS WEEK!

....

....

....

THIS WEEK'S GOALS

><> ....

><> ....

><> ....

PRIORITIES

><> ....

><> ....

><> ....

><> ....

PRAYER CONCERNS

><> ....

><> ....

><> ....

><> ....

GIVE THANKS FOR

><> ....

><> ....

><> ....

><> ....

MOUNTAIN MOVING Faith

Inspiring Quotes

"Faith is a living, daring confidence in God's grace, so sure and certain that a man could stake his life on it a thousand times."
— **Martin Luther**

"A grateful heart is a beginning of greatness. It is an expression of humility. It is a foundation for the development of such virtues as prayer, faith, courage, contentment, happiness, love, and well-being."
— **James E. Faust**

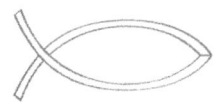

February

MOUNTAIN MOVING

Faith

Delivers Excellence

By faith Abel offered to God a more excellent sacrifice
than Cain, through which he obtained witness that he
was righteous, God testifying of his gifts; and through it
he being dead still speaks.
- Hebrews 11:4

Overview

sun	mon	tue	wed	thu	fri	sat
1	2	3	4	5	6	7
8	9	10	11	12	13	14
15	16 Presidents' Day	17	18	19	20	21
22	23	24	25	26	27	28

"Mountain Moving *Faith*" Note

Special Days

Week in View

Monday

Tuesday

Wednesday

Thursday

Friday

Weekend

Faith verse for the week:

But also for this very reason, giving all diligence, add to your faith virtue, to virtue knowledge.

2 Peter 1:5

Action Plan
for the Week

MOUNTAIN MOVING *Faith* FOCUS
FOR THIS WEEK!

....

....

....

THIS WEEK'S GOALS

✠ ....

✠ ....

✠ ....

PRIORITIES

✠ ....

✠ ....

✠ ....

✠ ....

PRAYER CONCERNS

✠ ....

✠ ....

✠ ....

✠ ....

GIVE THANKS FOR

✠ ....

✠ ....

✠ ....

✠ ....

Week in View

dates: **Monday, February 9** to **Sunday, February 15**

Monday	Tuesday	Wednesday

Thursday	Friday	Weekend

Faith verse for the week:

*But let him ask in faith, with no doubting, for he who doubts
is like a wave of the sea driven and tossed by the wind.*

James 1:6

Action Plan
for the Week

MOUNTAIN MOVING *Faith* FOCUS FOR THIS WEEK!

....

....

....

THIS WEEK'S GOALS

〉○ ....

〉○ ....

〉○ ....

PRIORITIES

〉○ ....

〉○ ....

〉○ ....

〉○ ....

PRAYER CONCERNS

〉○ ....

〉○ ....

〉○ ....

〉○ ....

GIVE THANKS FOR

〉○ ....

〉○ ....

〉○ ....

〉○ ....

Week in View

Monday	Tuesday	Wednesday

Thursday	Friday	Weekend

Faith verse for the week:

Above all, taking the shield of faith with which you will be able to quench all the fiery darts of the wicked one.
Ephesians 6:16

Action Plan
for the Week

MOUNTAIN MOVING *Faith* FOCUS
FOR THIS WEEK!

....
....
....

THIS WEEK'S GOALS

✦ ....
✦ ....
✦ ....

PRIORITIES

✦ ....
✦ ....
✦ ....
✦ ....

PRAYER CONCERNS

✦ ....
✦ ....
✦ ....
✦ ....

GIVE THANKS FOR

✦ ....
✦ ....
✦ ....
✦ ....
✦ ....

Week in View

Monday	Tuesday	Wednesday

Thursday	Friday	Weekend

Faith verse for the week:

*That your faith should not be in the wisdom of men
but in the power of God.*
1 Corinthians 2:5

Action Plan
for the Week

MOUNTAIN MOVING *Faith* FOCUS
FOR THIS WEEK!

....

....

....

THIS WEEK'S GOALS

✠ ....

✠ ....

✠ ....

PRIORITIES

✠ ....

✠ ....

✠ ....

✠ ....

PRAYER CONCERNS

✠ ....

✠ ....

✠ ....

✠ ....

GIVE THANKS FOR

✠ ....

✠ ....

✠ ....

✠ ....

MOUNTAIN MOVING *Faith*

Inspiring Quotes

"When you have faith in God, you don't have to worry about the future. You just know it's all in His hands. You just go to and do your best."
— **Elder Bryan Mathison**

"Through hard work, perseverance and a faith in God, you can live your dreams."
— **Ben Carson**

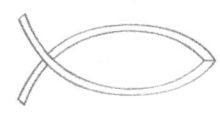

MARCH

MOUNTAIN MOVING

Faith

Pleases God

By faith Enoch was taken away so that he did not see death, "and was not found, because God had taken him"; for before he was taken he had this testimony, that he pleased God.
- Hebrews 11:5

Overview

month
March

year
2026

sun	mon	tue	wed	thu	fri	sat
1	2	3	4	5	6	7
8	9	10	11	12	13	14
15	16	17	18	19	20	21
22	23	24	25	26	27	28
29	30	31				

"Mountain Moving *Faith*" Note

Special Days

Week in View

dates: **Monday, March 2** to **Sunday, March 8**

Monday	Tuesday	Wednesday

Thursday	Friday	Weekend

Faith verse for the week:

Then behold, they brought to Him a paralytic lying on a bed. When Jesus saw their faith, He said to the paralytic, "Son, be of good cheer; your sins are forgiven you."
Matthew 9:2

Action Plan
for the Week

MOUNTAIN MOVING *Faith* FOCUS
FOR THIS WEEK!

··

··

··

THIS WEEK'S GOALS
><> ··
><> ··
><> ··

PRIORITIES
><> ··

><> ··

><> ··

><> ··

PRAYER CONCERNS
><> ··

><> ··

><> ··

><> ··

GIVE THANKS FOR
><> ··

><> ··

><> ··

><> ··

Week in View

dates: **Monday, March 9** to **Sunday, March 15**

Monday	Tuesday	Wednesday

Thursday	Friday	Weekend

Faith verse for the week:

Then Jesus answered and said to her, "O woman, great is your faith! Let it be to you as you desire." And her daughter was healed from that very hour.
Matthew 15:28

Action Plan
for the Week

MOUNTAIN MOVING *Faith* FOCUS
FOR THIS WEEK!

....

....

....

THIS WEEK'S GOALS

✙ ....

✙ ....

✙ ....

PRIORITIES

✙ ....

✙ ....

✙ ....

✙ ....

PRAYER CONCERNS

✙ ....

✙ ....

✙ ....

✙ ....

GIVE THANKS FOR

✙ ....

✙ ....

✙ ....

✙ ....

Week in View

Monday	Tuesday	Wednesday

Thursday	Friday	Weekend

Faith verse for the week:

*But you, O man of God, flee these things and pursue righteousness, godliness, **faith**, love, patience, gentleness.*
1 Timothy 6:11

Action Plan
for the Week

MOUNTAIN MOVING *Faith* FOCUS
FOR THIS WEEK!

....

....

....

THIS WEEK'S GOALS

> ....

> ....

> ....

PRIORITIES

> ....

> ....

> ....

> ....

PRAYER CONCERNS

> ....

> ....

> ....

GIVE THANKS FOR

> ....

> ....

> ....

> ....

Week in View

dates: Monday, March 23 to Sunday, March 29

Monday	**Tuesday**	**Wednesday**
Thursday	**Friday**	**Weekend**

Faith verse for the week:

*Let us draw near with a true heart in full assurance of faith,
having our hearts sprinkled from an evil conscience and our bodies
washed with pure water.*

Hebrews 10:22

Action Plan
for the Week

MOUNTAIN MOVING *Faith* FOCUS
FOR THIS WEEK!

....

....

....

THIS WEEK'S GOALS

⋈ ....

⋈ ....

⋈ ....

PRIORITIES

⋈ ....

⋈ ....

⋈ ....

⋈ ....

PRAYER CONCERNS

⋈ ....

⋈ ....

⋈ ....

⋈ ....

GIVE THANKS FOR

⋈ ....

⋈ ....

⋈ ....

⋈ ....

⋈ ....

Week in View

dates: **Monday, March 30** to **Tuesday, March 31**

Monday	Tuesday	

Faith verse for the week:

So the Lord said, "If you have faith as a mustard seed, you can say to this mulberry tree, 'Be pulled up by the roots and be planted in the sea,' and it would obey you.
Luke 17:6

Action Plan
for the Week

MOUNTAIN MOVING *Faith* FOCUS
FOR THIS WEEK!

....

....

....

THIS WEEK'S GOALS

✠ ....

✠ ....

✠ ....

PRIORITIES

✠ ....

✠ ....

✠ ....

✠ ....

PRAYER CONCERNS

✠ ....

✠ ....

✠ ....

✠ ....

GIVE THANKS FOR

✠ ....

✠ ....

✠ ....

✠ ....

MOUNTAIN MOVING Faith

Inspiring Quotes

"Every day you need to get a full dose of the Word and meditate on scripture, and if you discipline yourself and remain consistent, your faith will grow and mature, and remember that God, the Word, and your faith, is a recipe for success."
— Stephanie Williams

"True faith rests upon the character of God and asks no further proof than the moral perfections of the One who cannot lie."
— A.W. Tozer

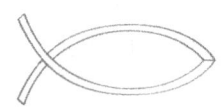

APRIL

MOUNTAIN
MOVING

Faith

Sees the Unseen

By faith Noah, being divinely warned of things not yet
seen, moved with godly fear, prepared an ark for the
saving of his household.
- Hebrews 11:7

Overview

sun	mon	tue	wed	thu	fri	sat
			1	2	3 Good Friday	4
5	6 Easter Monday	7	8	9	10	11
12	13	14	15	16	17	18
19	20	21	22	23	24	25
26	27	28	29	30		

"Mountain Moving *Faith*" Note

Special Days

Week in View

dates: **Wednesday, April 1 to Sunday, April 5**

		Wednesday
Thursday	**Friday**	**Weekend**

Faith verse for the week:

Now faith is the substance of things hoped for, the evidence of things not seen.

Hebrews 11:1

Action Plan
for the Week

MOUNTAIN MOVING *Faith* FOCUS
FOR THIS WEEK!

....

....

....

THIS WEEK'S GOALS

><> ....

><> ....

><> ....

PRIORITIES

><> ....

><> ....

><> ....

><> ....

PRAYER CONCERNS

><> ....

><> ....

><> ....

><> ....

GIVE THANKS FOR

><> ....

><> ....

><> ....

><> ....

><> ....

Week in View

dates: **Monday, April 6** to **Sunday, April 12**

Monday	Tuesday	Wednesday

Thursday	Friday	Weekend

Faith verse for the week:

"If you have faith as a mustard seed, you will say to this mountain, 'Move from here to there,' and it will move; and nothing will be impossible for you."
Matthew 17:20b

Action Plan
for the Week

MOUNTAIN MOVING *Faith* FOCUS
FOR THIS WEEK!

....

....

....

THIS WEEK'S GOALS

> ....

> ....

> ....

PRIORITIES

> ....

> ....

> ....

> ....

PRAYER CONCERNS

> ....

> ....

> ....

> ....

GIVE THANKS FOR

> ....

> ....

> ....

> ....

Week in View

Monday	Tuesday	Wednesday

Thursday	Friday	Weekend

Faith verse for the week:

By faith he (Moses: emphasis added) forsook Egypt, not fearing the wrath of the king; for he endured as seeing Him who is invisible.
Hebrews 11:27

Action Plan
for the Week

MOUNTAIN MOVING *Faith* FOCUS
FOR THIS WEEK!

....
....
....

THIS WEEK'S GOALS

>< ....
>< ....
>< ....

PRIORITIES

>< ....
>< ....
>< ....
>< ....

PRAYER CONCERNS

>< ....
>< ....
>< ....
>< ....

GIVE THANKS FOR

>< ....
>< ....
>< ....
>< ....

Week in View

dates: **Monday, April 20** to **Sunday, April 26**

Monday	Tuesday	Wednesday

Thursday	Friday	Weekend

Faith verse for the week:

Though now you do not see Him, yet believing, you rejoice with joy inexpressible and full of glory, receiving the end of your faith—the salvation of your souls.
1 Peter 1:8b-9

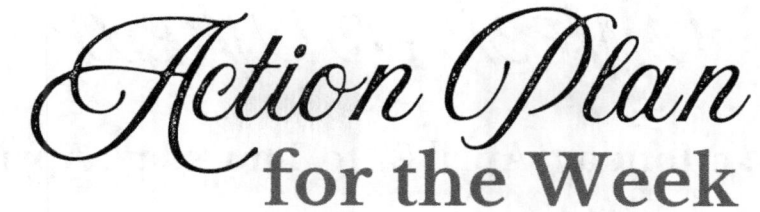

Action Plan
for the Week

MOUNTAIN MOVING *Faith* FOCUS
FOR THIS WEEK!

....

....

....

THIS WEEK'S GOALS

- ....
- ....
- ....

PRIORITIES

- ....
- ....
- ....
- ....

PRAYER CONCERNS

- ....
- ....
- ....
- ....

GIVE THANKS FOR

- ....
- ....
- ....
- ....

Week in View

dates: Monday, April 27 to Thursday, April 30

Monday	Tuesday	Wednesday

Thursday		

Faith verse for the week:

"And whatever things you ask in prayer, believing, you will receive."
Matthew 21:22

Action Plan
for the Week

MOUNTAIN MOVING *Faith* FOCUS
FOR THIS WEEK!

....

....

....

THIS WEEK'S GOALS

◠ ....

◠ ....

◠ ....

PRIORITIES

◠ ....

◠ ....

◠ ....

◠ ....

PRAYER CONCERNS

◠ ....

◠ ....

◠ ....

◠ ....

GIVE THANKS FOR

◠ ....

◠ ....

◠ ....

◠ ....

◠ ....

MOUNTAIN MOVING Faith

Inspiring Quotes

"Faith is unseen but felt, faith is strength when we feel we have none, faith is hope when all seems lost."
— Catherine Pulsifer

"Faith is to believe what you do not see; the reward of this faith is to see what you believe."
— Saint Augustine

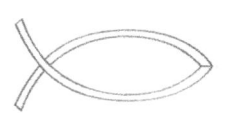

May

MOUNTAIN MOVING

Faith

Is Obedient

By faith Abraham obeyed when he was called to go out
to the place which he would receive as an inheritance.
And he went out, not knowing where he was going.
- Hebrews 11:8

Overview

sun	mon	tue	wed	thu	fri	sat
					1	2
3	4	5	6	7	8	9
10	11	12	13	14	15	16
17	18	19	20	21	22	23
24/31	25 **Memorial Day** Whit Monday	26	27	28	29	30

"Mountain Moving Faith" Note

Special Days

Week in View

dates: Friday, May 1 to Sunday, May 3

Friday

Weekend

Faith verse for the week:

So then faith comes by hearing, and hearing by the word of God.
Romans 10:17

Action Plan
for the Week

MOUNTAIN MOVING *Faith* FOCUS
FOR THIS WEEK!

....

....

....

THIS WEEK'S GOALS

- ....
- ....
- ....

PRIORITIES

- ....
- ....
- ....
- ....

PRAYER CONCERNS

- ....
- ....
- ....
- ....

GIVE THANKS FOR

- ....
- ....
- ....
- ....

Week in View

dates: Monday, May 4 to Sunday, May 10

Monday

Tuesday

Wednesday

Thursday

Friday

Weekend

Faith verse for the week:

*Through Him we have received grace and apostleship for obedience
to the faith among all nations for His name.*
Romans 1:5

Action Plan
for the Week

MOUNTAIN MOVING *Faith* FOCUS
FOR THIS WEEK!

....

....

....

THIS WEEK'S GOALS

✝ ....

✝ ....

✝ ....

PRIORITIES

✝ ....

✝ ....

✝ ....

✝ ....

PRAYER CONCERNS

✝ ....

✝ ....

✝ ....

✝ ....

GIVE THANKS FOR

✝ ....

✝ ....

✝ ....

✝ ....

✝ ....

Week in View

dates: **Monday, May 11** to **Sunday, May 17**

Monday	Tuesday	Wednesday

Thursday	Friday	Weekend

Faith verse for the week:

Jesus said to him, "If you can believe, all things are possible to him who believes."
Mark 9:23

Action Plan
for the Week

MOUNTAIN MOVING *Faith* FOCUS
FOR THIS WEEK!

....
....
....

THIS WEEK'S GOALS

>◦ ....
>◦ ....
>◦ ....

PRIORITIES

>◦ ....
>◦ ....
>◦ ....
>◦ ....

PRAYER CONCERNS

>◦ ....
>◦ ....
>◦ ....
>◦ ....

GIVE THANKS FOR

>◦ ....
>◦ ....
>◦ ....
>◦ ....
>◦ ....

Week in View

Monday	Tuesday	Wednesday

Thursday	Friday	Weekend

Faith verse for the week:

For by grace you have been saved through faith, and that not of yourselves; it is the gift of God.
Ephesians 2:8

Action Plan
for the Week

MOUNTAIN MOVING *Faith* FOCUS
FOR THIS WEEK!

....

....

....

THIS WEEK'S GOALS

⋈ ....

⋈ ....

⋈ ....

PRIORITIES

⋈ ....

⋈ ....

⋈ ....

⋈ ....

PRAYER CONCERNS

⋈ ....

⋈ ....

⋈ ....

⋈ ....

GIVE THANKS FOR

⋈ ....

⋈ ....

⋈ ....

⋈ ....

Week in View

dates: Monday, May 25 to Sunday, May 31

Monday	Tuesday	Wednesday

Thursday	Friday	Weekend

Faith verse for the week:

For as the body without the spirit is dead, so faith without works is dead also.
James 2:26

Action Plan
for the Week

MOUNTAIN MOVING *Faith* FOCUS
FOR THIS WEEK!

....

....

....

THIS WEEK'S GOALS

>< ....

>< ....

>< ....

PRIORITIES

>< ....

>< ....

>< ....

>< ....

PRAYER CONCERNS

>< ....

>< ....

>< ....

>< ....

GIVE THANKS FOR

>< ....

>< ....

>< ....

>< ....

MOUNTAIN MOVING *Faith*

Inspiring Quotes

"I believe if you keep your faith, you keep your trust, you keep the right attitude, if you're grateful, you'll see God open up new doors."
— **Joel Osteen**

"Every single thing He has ever or will ever say is true. The simplicity of faith is this: taking God's Word for it."
— **Jackie Hill Perry**

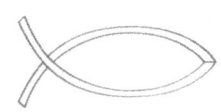

JUNE

MOUNTAIN
MOVING
Faith

Does the Impossible

By faith Sarah herself also received strength to conceive seed, and she bore a child when she was past the age, because she judged Him faithful who had promised. 12 Therefore from one man, and him as good as dead, were born as many as the stars of the sky in multitude —innumerable as the sand which is by the seashore.
- Hebrews 11:11-12

Overview

month: June
year: 2026

sun	mon	tue	wed	thu	fri	sat
	1	2	3	4	5 Randol Fawkes Labour Day	6
7	8	9	10	11	12	13
14	15	16	17	18	19 Juneteenth	20
21	22	23	24	25	26	27
28	29	30				

"Mountain Moving *Faith*" Note

Special Days

Week in View

dates: Monday, June 1 to Sunday, June 7

Monday	Tuesday	Wednesday

Thursday	Friday	Weekend

Faith verse for the week:

"For with God nothing will be impossible."
Luke 1:37

Action Plan
for the Week

MOUNTAIN MOVING *Faith* FOCUS
FOR THIS WEEK!

....

....

....

THIS WEEK'S GOALS

✦ ....

✦ ....

✦ ....

PRIORITIES

✦ ....

✦ ....

✦ ....

✦ ....

PRAYER CONCERNS

✦ ....

✦ ....

✦ ....

✦ ....

GIVE THANKS FOR

✦ ....

✦ ....

✦ ....

✦ ....

Week in View

Monday	Tuesday	Wednesday

Thursday	Friday	Weekend

Faith verse for the week:

I can do all things through Christ who strengthens me.
Philippians 4:13

Action Plan
for the Week

MOUNTAIN MOVING *Faith* FOCUS
FOR THIS WEEK!

....
....
....

THIS WEEK'S GOALS

><> ....
><> ....
><> ....

PRIORITIES

><> ....
><> ....
><> ....
><> ....

PRAYER CONCERNS

><> ....
><> ....
><> ....
><> ....

GIVE THANKS FOR

><> ....
><> ....
><> ....
><> ....

Week in View

dates: **Monday, June 15** to **Sunday, June 21**

Monday	**Tuesday**	**Wednesday**

Thursday	**Friday**	**Weekend**

Faith verse for the week:

"Assuredly, I say to you, if you have faith and do not doubt, you will not only do what was done to the fig tree, but also if you say to this mountain, 'Be removed and be cast into the sea,' it will be done."

Matthew 21:21b

Action Plan
for the Week

MOUNTAIN MOVING *Faith* FOCUS
FOR THIS WEEK!

....

....

....

THIS WEEK'S GOALS

><> ....

><> ....

><> ....

PRIORITIES

><> ....

><> ....

><> ....

><> ....

PRAYER CONCERNS

><> ....

><> ....

><> ....

><> ....

GIVE THANKS FOR

><> ....

><> ....

><> ....

><> ....

Week in View

dates: Monday, June 22 to Sunday, June 28

Monday

Tuesday

Wednesday

Thursday

Friday

Weekend

Faith verse for the week:

Now to Him who is able to do exceedingly abundantly above all that we ask or think, according to the power that works in us.
Ephesians 3:20

Action Plan
for the Week

MOUNTAIN MOVING *Faith* FOCUS
FOR THIS WEEK!

....

....

....

THIS WEEK'S GOALS

>◦ ....

>◦ ....

>◦ ....

PRIORITIES

>◦ ....

>◦ ....

>◦ ....

>◦ ....

PRAYER CONCERNS

>◦ ....

>◦ ....

>◦ ....

>◦ ....

GIVE THANKS FOR

>◦ ....

>◦ ....

>◦ ....

>◦ ....

Week in View

dates: Monday, June 29 to Tuesday, June 30

Monday	Tuesday	

Faith verse for the week:

"Most assuredly, I say to you, he who believes in Me, the works that I do he will do also; and greater works than these he will do, because I go to My Father."
John 14:12

Action Plan
for the Week

MOUNTAIN MOVING *Faith* FOCUS
FOR THIS WEEK!

....

....

....

THIS WEEK'S GOALS

✠ ....

✠ ....

✠ ....

PRIORITIES

✠ ....

✠ ....

✠ ....

✠ ....

PRAYER CONCERNS

✠ ....

✠ ....

✠ ....

✠ ....

GIVE THANKS FOR

✠ ....

✠ ....

✠ ....

✠ ....

MOUNTAIN MOVING Faith

Inspiring Quotes

"Faith is the strength by which a shattered world shall emerge into the light."
— **Helen Keller**

"Faith consists in believing when it is beyond the power of reason to believe."
— **Voltaire**

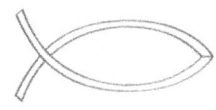

JULY

MOUNTAIN
MOVING

Faith

Sees the Future

By faith Isaac blessed Jacob and Esau concerning things
to come.
- Hebrews 11:20

Overview

month

July

year

2026

sun	mon	tue	wed	thu	fri	sat
			1	2	3 Independence Day Observed (US)	4 Independence Day (US)
5	6	7	8	9	10 Independence Day (BS)	11
12	13	14	15	16	17	18
19	20	21	22	23	24	25
26	27	28	29	30	31	

"Mountain Moving *Faith*" Note

Special Days

Week in View

dates: Wednesday, July 1 to Sunday, July 5

		Wednesday

Thursday	**Friday**	**Weekend**

Faith verse for the week:

Therefore I say to you, whatever things you ask when you pray,
believe that you receive them, and you will have them.
Mark 11:24

Action Plan
for the Week

MOUNTAIN MOVING *Faith* FOCUS
FOR THIS WEEK!

....

....

....

THIS WEEK'S GOALS

>○ ....

>○ ....

>○ ....

PRIORITIES

>○ ....

>○ ....

>○ ....

>○ ....

PRAYER CONCERNS

>○ ....

>○ ....

>○ ....

>○ ....

GIVE THANKS FOR

>○ ....

>○ ....

>○ ....

>○ ....

>○ ....

Week in View

Monday	Tuesday	Wednesday

Thursday	Friday	Weekend

Faith verse for the week:

I have been crucified with Christ; it is no longer I who live, but Christ lives in me; and the life which I now live in the flesh I live by faith in the Son of God, who loved me and gave Himself for me.

Galatians 2:20

Action Plan
for the Week

MOUNTAIN MOVING *Faith* FOCUS
FOR THIS WEEK!

....

....

....

THIS WEEK'S GOALS

> ....

> ....

> ....

PRIORITIES

> ....

> ....

> ....

> ....

PRAYER CONCERNS

> ....

> ....

> ....

> ....

GIVE THANKS FOR

> ....

> ....

> ....

> ....

Week in View

dates: Monday, July 13 to Sunday, July 19

Monday	Tuesday	Wednesday

Thursday	Friday	Weekend

Faith verse for the week:

Your word is a lamp to my feet And a light to my path.
Psalm 119:105

Action Plan
for the Week

MOUNTAIN MOVING *Faith* FOCUS
FOR THIS WEEK!

....

....

....

THIS WEEK'S GOALS

><> ....

><> ....

><> ....

PRIORITIES

><> ....

><> ....

><> ....

><> ....

PRAYER CONCERNS

><> ....

><> ....

><> ....

><> ....

GIVE THANKS FOR

><> ....

><> ....

><> ....

><> ....

Week in View

dates: Monday, July 20 to Sunday, July 26

Monday	Tuesday	Wednesday

Thursday	Friday	Weekend

Faith verse for the week:

Trust in the Lord with all your heart, And lean not on your own understanding.
Proverbs 3:5

Action Plan
for the Week

MOUNTAIN MOVING *Faith* FOCUS
FOR THIS WEEK!

....

....

....

THIS WEEK'S GOALS

><> ....

><> ....

><> ....

PRIORITIES

><> ....

><> ....

><> ....

><> ....

PRAYER CONCERNS

><> ....

><> ....

><> ....

><> ....

GIVE THANKS FOR

><> ....

><> ....

><> ....

><> ....

Week in View

dates: Monday, July 27 to Sunday, August 2

Monday	Tuesday	Wednesday

Thursday	Friday	Weekend

Faith verse for the week:

In all your ways acknowledge Him, And He shall direct your paths.
Proverbs 3:6

Action Plan
for the Week

MOUNTAIN MOVING *Faith* FOCUS
FOR THIS WEEK!

....

....

....

THIS WEEK'S GOALS

✞ ....

✞ ....

✞ ....

PRIORITIES

✞ ....

✞ ....

✞ ....

✞ ....

PRAYER CONCERNS

✞ ....

✞ ....

✞ ....

GIVE THANKS FOR

✞ ....

✞ ....

✞ ....

✞ ....

MOUNTAIN MOVING Faith

Inspiring Quotes

"No matter what has happened to you in the past or what is going on in your life right now, it has no power to keep you from having an amazingly good future if you will walk by faith in God. God loves you! He wants you to live with victory over sin so you can possess His promises for your life today!"
— **Joyce Meyer**

"Faith is taking the first step even when you don't see the whole staircase."
— **Martin Luther King, Jr.**

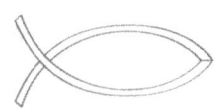

August

MOUNTAIN MOVING
Faith

Blesses and Worships

By faith Jacob, when he was dying, blessed each of the sons of Joseph, and worshiped, leaning on the top of his staff.
- Hebrews 11:21

Overview

sun	mon	tue	wed	thu	fri	sat
						1
2	3 Emancipation Day	4	5	6	7	8
9	10	11	12	13	14	15
16	17	18	19	20	21	22
23/30	24/31	25	26	27	28	29

"Mountain Moving *Faith*" Note

Special Days

Week in View

dates: Monday, August 3 to Sunday, August 9

Monday	Tuesday	Wednesday

Thursday	Friday	Weekend

Faith verse for the week:

I beseech you therefore, brethren, by the mercies of God, that you present your bodies a living sacrifice, holy, acceptable to God, which is your reasonable service.

Romans 12:1

Action Plan for the Week

MOUNTAIN MOVING *Faith* FOCUS FOR THIS WEEK!

THIS WEEK'S GOALS

PRIORITIES

PRAYER CONCERNS

GIVE THANKS FOR

Week in View

Monday	Tuesday	Wednesday

Thursday	Friday	Weekend

Faith verse for the week:

Oh come, let us worship and bow down; Let us kneel before the Lord our Maker.

Psalm 95:6

Action Plan
for the Week

MOUNTAIN MOVING *Faith* FOCUS
FOR THIS WEEK!

....

....

....

THIS WEEK'S GOALS

✺ ....

✺ ....

✺ ....

PRIORITIES

✺ ....

✺ ....

✺ ....

✺ ....

PRAYER CONCERNS

✺ ....

✺ ....

✺ ....

✺ ....

GIVE THANKS FOR

✺ ....

✺ ....

✺ ....

✺ ....

Week in View

dates: Monday, August 17 to Sunday, August 23

Monday	Tuesday	Wednesday

Thursday	Friday	Weekend

Faith verse for the week:

*Above all, taking the shield of faith with which you will be able
to quench all the fiery darts of the wicked one.*
Ephesians 6:16

Action Plan
for the Week

MOUNTAIN MOVING *Faith* FOCUS
FOR THIS WEEK!

....

....

....

THIS WEEK'S GOALS

> ....

> ....

> ....

PRIORITIES

> ....

> ....

> ....

> ....

PRAYER CONCERNS

> ....

> ....

> ....

> ....

GIVE THANKS FOR

> ....

> ....

> ....

> ....

> ....

Week in View

dates: Monday, August 24 to Sunday, August 30

Monday	Tuesday	Wednesday

Thursday	Friday	Weekend

Faith verse for the week:

Give to the Lord the glory due His name; Bring an offering, and come before Him. Oh, worship the Lord in the beauty of holiness!
1 Chronicles 16:29

Action Plan
for the Week

MOUNTAIN MOVING *Faith* FOCUS
FOR THIS WEEK!

....

....

....

THIS WEEK'S GOALS

>< ....

>< ....

>< ....

PRIORITIES

>< ....

>< ....

>< ....

>< ....

PRAYER CONCERNS

>< ....

>< ....

>< ....

>< ....

GIVE THANKS FOR

>< ....

>< ....

>< ....

>< ....

>< ....

Week in View

date: Monday, August 31

Monday

Action Plan
for the Week

MOUNTAIN MOVING *Faith* FOCUS
FOR THIS WEEK!

....

....

....

THIS WEEK'S GOALS

✦ ....

✦ ....

✦ ....

PRIORITIES

✦ ....

✦ ....

✦ ....

✦ ....

PRAYER CONCERNS

✦ ....

✦ ....

✦ ....

✦ ....

GIVE THANKS FOR

✦ ....

✦ ....

✦ ....

✦ ....

MOUNTAIN MOVING Faith

Inspiring Quotes

"The greatest legacy one can pass on to one's children and grandchildren is not money or other material things accumulated in one's life, but rather a legacy of character and faith."
— **Billy Graham**

"It is a blessing for our children to see us live out our faith—trusting in God's good character and provision—even when we don't have all the answers."
— **Marissa Bondurant**

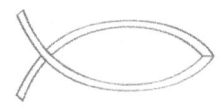

SEPTEMBER

MOUNTAIN MOVING

Faith

Divinely Declares

By faith Joseph, when he was dying, made mention of
the departure of the children of Israel, and gave
instructions concerning his bones.
- Hebrews 11:22

Overview

sun	mon	tue	wed	thu	fri	sat
		1	2	3	4	5
6	7 Labor Day	8	9	10	11	12
13	14	15	16	17	18	19
20	21	22	23	24	25	26
27	28	29	30			

"Mountain Moving *Faith*" Note

Special Days

Week in View

dates: **Tuesday, September 1** to **Sunday, September 6**

	Tuesday	**Wednesday**

Thursday	**Friday**	**Weekend**

Faith verse for the week:

*But that no one is justified by the law in the sight of God is
evident, for "the just shall live by faith."*
Galatians 3:11

Action Plan
for the Week

MOUNTAIN MOVING *Faith* FOCUS
FOR THIS WEEK!

....

....

....

THIS WEEK'S GOALS

> ....

> ....

> ....

PRIORITIES

> ....

> ....

> ....

> ....

PRAYER CONCERNS

> ....

> ....

> ....

> ....

GIVE THANKS FOR

> ....

> ....

> ....

> ....

Week in View

dates: Monday, September 7 to Sunday, September 13

Monday	Tuesday	Wednesday

Thursday	Friday	Weekend

Faith verse for the week:

He did not waver at the promise of God through unbelief, but was strengthened in faith, giving glory to God, and being fully convinced that what He had promised He was also able to perform.
Romans 4:20-21

Action Plan
for the Week

MOUNTAIN MOVING *Faith* FOCUS
FOR THIS WEEK!

....

....

....

THIS WEEK'S GOALS

◇ ....

◇ ....

◇ ....

PRIORITIES

◇ ....

◇ ....

◇ ....

◇ ....

PRAYER CONCERNS

◇ ....

◇ ....

◇ ....

◇ ....

GIVE THANKS FOR

◇ ....

◇ ....

◇ ....

◇ ....

◇ ....

Week in View

Monday	Tuesday	Wednesday

Thursday	Friday	Weekend

Faith verse for the week:

*And since we have the same spirit of faith, according to what is written,
"I believed and therefore I spoke," we also believe and therefore speak.*
2 Corinthians 4:13

Action Plan
for the Week

MOUNTAIN MOVING *Faith* FOCUS
FOR THIS WEEK!

....

....

....

THIS WEEK'S GOALS

>< ....

>< ....

>< ....

PRIORITIES

>< ....

>< ....

>< ....

>< ....

PRAYER CONCERNS

>< ....

>< ....

>< ....

>< ....

GIVE THANKS FOR

>< ....

>< ....

>< ....

>< ....

Week in View

Monday	Tuesday	Wednesday

Thursday	Friday	Weekend

Faith verse for the week:

For whatever is born of God overcomes the world. And this is
the victory that has overcome the world—our faith.
1 John 5:4

Action Plan
for the Week

MOUNTAIN MOVING *Faith* FOCUS
FOR THIS WEEK!

....

....

....

THIS WEEK'S GOALS

>< ....

>< ....

>< ....

PRIORITIES

>< ....

>< ....

>< ....

>< ....

PRAYER CONCERNS

>< ....

>< ....

>< ....

>< ....

GIVE THANKS FOR

>< ....

>< ....

>< ....

>< ....

Week in View

dates: **Monday, September 28** to **Wednesday, September 30**

Monday	Tuesday	Wednesday

Faith verse for the week:

Therefore, having been justified by faith, we have peace with God through our Lord Jesus Christ.

Romans 5:1

Action Plan
for the Week

MOUNTAIN MOVING *Faith* FOCUS
FOR THIS WEEK!

....

....

....

THIS WEEK'S GOALS

⋈ ....

⋈ ....

⋈ ....

PRIORITIES

⋈ ....

⋈ ....

⋈ ....

⋈ ....

PRAYER CONCERNS

⋈ ....

⋈ ....

⋈ ....

⋈ ....

GIVE THANKS FOR

⋈ ....

⋈ ....

⋈ ....

⋈ ....

MOUNTAIN MOVING *Faith*

Inspiring Quotes

"Faith is not believing in my own unshakable belief. Faith is believing an unshakable God when everything in me trembles and quakes."
— **Beth Moore**

"Never be afraid to trust an unknown future to a known God."
— **Corrie ten Boom**

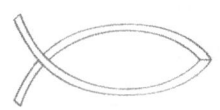

OCTOBER

MOUNTAIN MOVING

Faith

Detects Beauty

By faith Moses, when he was born, was hidden three
months by his parents, because they saw he was a
beautiful child; and they were not afraid of the king's
command.
- Hebrews 11:23

Overview

month
October

year
2026

sun	mon	tue	wed	thu	fri	sat
				1	2	3
4	5	6	7	8	9	10
11	12 **Columbus Day** National Heroes Day	13	14	15	16	17
18	19	20	21	22	23	24
25	26	27	28	29	30	31

"Mountain Moving *Faith*" Note

Special Days

Week in View

dates: **Thursday, October 1** to **Sunday, October 4**

Thursday	Friday	Weekend

Faith verse for the week:

But as it is written: "Eye has not seen, nor ear heard, Nor have entered into the heart of man The things which God has prepared for those who love Him."
1 Corinthians 2:9

Action Plan
for the Week

MOUNTAIN MOVING *Faith* FOCUS
FOR THIS WEEK!

....

....

....

THIS WEEK'S GOALS

>< ....

>< ....

>< ....

PRIORITIES

>< ....

>< ....

>< ....

>< ....

PRAYER CONCERNS

>< ....

>< ....

>< ....

>< ....

GIVE THANKS FOR

>< ....

>< ....

>< ....

>< ....

Week in View

dates: **Monday, October 5** to **Sunday, October 11**

Monday	Tuesday	Wednesday

Thursday	Friday	Weekend

Faith verse for the week:

The heavens declare the glory of God; And the firmament shows His handiwork.
Psalm 19:1

Action Plan
for the Week

MOUNTAIN MOVING *Faith* FOCUS
FOR THIS WEEK!

....

....

....

THIS WEEK'S GOALS

❧ ....

❧ ....

❧ ....

PRIORITIES

❧ ....

❧ ....

❧ ....

❧ ....

PRAYER CONCERNS

❧ ....

❧ ....

❧ ....

❧ ....

GIVE THANKS FOR

❧ ....

❧ ....

❧ ....

❧ ....

❧ ....

Week in View

Monday	Tuesday	Wednesday

Thursday	Friday	Weekend

Faith verse for the week:

One thing I have desired of the Lord, That will I seek: That I may dwell in the house of the Lord All the days of my life, To behold the beauty of the Lord, And to inquire in His temple.

Psalm 27:4

Action Plan
for the Week

MOUNTAIN MOVING *Faith* FOCUS
FOR THIS WEEK!

....

....

....

THIS WEEK'S GOALS

><> ....

><> ....

><> ....

PRIORITIES

><> ....

><> ....

><> ....

><> ....

PRAYER CONCERNS

><> ....

><> ....

><> ....

><> ....

GIVE THANKS FOR

><> ....

><> ....

><> ....

><> ....

Week in View

dates: **Monday, October 19** to **Sunday, October 25**

Monday	**Tuesday**	**Wednesday**

Thursday	**Friday**	**Weekend**

Faith verse for the week:

Whom having not seen you love. Though now you do not see Him, yet believing, you rejoice with joy inexpressible and full of glory.
1 Peter 1:8

Action Plan
for the Week

MOUNTAIN MOVING *Faith* FOCUS
FOR THIS WEEK!

....

....

....

THIS WEEK'S GOALS

- ....
- ....
- ....

PRIORITIES

- ....
- ....
- ....
- ....

PRAYER CONCERNS

- ....
- ....
- ....
- ....

GIVE THANKS FOR

- ....
- ....
- ....
- ....

Week in View

dates: **Monday, October 26** to **Sunday, November 1**

Monday	Tuesday	Wednesday

Thursday	Friday	Weekend

Faith verse for the week:

I will praise You, for I am fearfully and wonderfully made; Marvelous are Your works, And that my soul knows very well.
Psalm 139:14

Action Plan
for the Week

MOUNTAIN MOVING *Faith* FOCUS
FOR THIS WEEK!

....

....

....

THIS WEEK'S GOALS

>< ....

>< ....

>< ....

PRIORITIES

>< ....

>< ....

>< ....

>< ....

PRAYER CONCERNS

>< ....

>< ....

>< ....

GIVE THANKS FOR

>< ....

>< ....

>< ....

>< ....

>< ....

MOUNTAIN
MOVING
Faith

Inspiring Quotes

"All I have seen teaches me to trust the Creator for all I have not seen."
— **Ralph Waldo Emerson**

"Faith is not the belief that God will do what you want. It is the belief that God will do what is right."
— **Max Lucado**

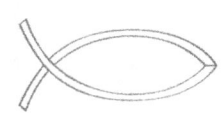

November

MOUNTAIN
MOVING
Faith

Breaks Down Walls

By faith the walls of Jericho fell down after they were
encircled for seven days.
- Hebrews 11:30

Overview

sun	mon	tue	wed	thu	fri	sat
1	2	3	4	5	6	7
8	9	10	11 Veterans Day	12	13	14
15	16	17	18	19	20	21
22	23	24	25	26 Thanksgiving Day	27	28
29	30					

"Mountain Moving Faith" Note

Special Days

Week in View

dates: Monday, November 2 to Sunday, November 8

Monday	Tuesday	Wednesday

Thursday	Friday	Weekend

Faith verse for the week:

For He Himself is our peace, who has made both one, and has broken down the middle wall of separation.
Ephesians 2:14

Action Plan
for the Week

MOUNTAIN MOVING *Faith* FOCUS
FOR THIS WEEK!

....

....

....

THIS WEEK'S GOALS

><> ....

><> ....

><> ....

PRIORITIES

><> ....

><> ....

><> ....

><> ....

PRAYER CONCERNS

><> ....

><> ....

><> ....

><> ....

GIVE THANKS FOR

><> ....

><> ....

><> ....

><> ....

><> ....

Week in View

dates: **Monday, November 9** to **Sunday, November 15**

Monday	Tuesday	Wednesday

Thursday	Friday	Weekend

Faith verse for the week:

So Jesus answered and said to them, "Have faith in God. For assuredly, I say to you, whoever says to this mountain, 'Be removed and be cast into the sea,' and does not doubt in his heart, but believes that those things he says will be done, he will have whatever he says."

Mark 11:22-23

Action Plan
for the Week

MOUNTAIN MOVING *Faith* FOCUS
FOR THIS WEEK!

....
....
....

THIS WEEK'S GOALS

✤ ....
✤ ....
✤ ....

PRIORITIES

✤ ....
✤ ....
✤ ....
✤ ....

PRAYER CONCERNS

✤ ....
✤ ....
✤ ....

GIVE THANKS FOR

✤ ....
✤ ....
✤ ....
✤ ....

Week in View

dates: **Monday, November 16** to **Sunday, November 22**

Monday	Tuesday	Wednesday

Thursday	Friday	Weekend

Faith verse for the week:

But at midnight Paul and Silas were praying and singing hymns to God, and the prisoners were listening to them. Suddenly there was a great earthquake, so that the foundations of the prison were shaken; and immediately all the doors were opened and everyone's chains were loosed.

Acts 16:25-26

Action Plan
for the Week

MOUNTAIN MOVING *Faith* FOCUS
FOR THIS WEEK!

....

....

....

THIS WEEK'S GOALS

✺ ....

✺ ....

✺ ....

PRIORITIES

✺ ....

✺ ....

✺ ....

✺ ....

PRAYER CONCERNS

✺ ....

✺ ....

✺ ....

✺ ....

GIVE THANKS FOR

✺ ....

✺ ....

✺ ....

✺ ....

✺ ....

Week in View

dates: **Monday, November 23** to **Sunday, November 29**

Monday	Tuesday	Wednesday

Thursday	Friday	Weekend

Faith verse for the week:

For by You I can run against a troop, By my God I can leap over a wall.
Psalm 18:29

Action Plan
for the Week

MOUNTAIN MOVING *Faith* FOCUS
FOR THIS WEEK!

....

....

....

THIS WEEK'S GOALS

⊱⊰ ....

⊱⊰ ....

⊱⊰ ....

PRIORITIES

⊱⊰ ....

⊱⊰ ....

⊱⊰ ....

⊱⊰ ....

PRAYER CONCERNS

⊱⊰ ....

⊱⊰ ....

⊱⊰ ....

⊱⊰ ....

GIVE THANKS FOR

⊱⊰ ....

⊱⊰ ....

⊱⊰ ....

⊱⊰ ....

⊱⊰ ....

Week in View

date: **Monday, November 30**

Monday

Faith verse for the week:

Watch, stand fast in the faith, be brave, be strong.
1 Corinthians 16:13

Action Plan
for the Week

MOUNTAIN MOVING *Faith* FOCUS
FOR THIS WEEK!

....

....

....

THIS WEEK'S GOALS

....

....

....

PRIORITIES

....

....

....

....

PRAYER CONCERNS

....

....

....

....

GIVE THANKS FOR

....

....

....

....

MOUNTAIN MOVING Faith

Inspiring Quotes

"We can look at Job, we can look at Lamentations, we can look at the Psalms, we can look at so many heroes of the faith who at different times had questions, who faced unbelief, yet God kept them, and they continued, in their doubts, to lean towards God, to lean and doubt in a way that continued to keep them attached to the vine and seeking Jesus in all of it."
— Laura Wifler

"I believe that God has put gifts and talents and ability on the inside of every one of us. When you develop that and you believe in yourself and you believe that you're a person of influence and a person of purpose, I believe you can rise up out of any situation."
— Joel Osteen

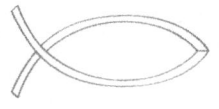

DECEMBER

MOUNTAIN MOVING
Faith

Redeems and Saves

By faith the harlot Rahab did not perish with those who did not believe, when she had received the spies with peace.
- Hebrews 11:31

Overview

sun	mon	tue	wed	thu	fri	sat
		1	2	3	4	5
6	7	8	9	10	11	12
13	14	15	16	17	18	19
20	21	22	23	24	25 Christmas Day (US & BS)	26 Boxing Day
27	28	29	30	31		

"Mountain Moving Faith" Note

Special Days

Week in View

dates: **Tuesday, December 1** to **Sunday, December 6**

	Tuesday	**Wednesday**
Thursday	**Friday**	**Weekend**

Faith verse for the week:

Christ has redeemed us from the curse of the law, having become a curse for us (for it is written, "Cursed is everyone who hangs on a tree"), that the blessing of Abraham might come upon the Gentiles in Christ Jesus, that we might receive the promise of the Spirit through faith.
Galatians 3:13-14

Action Plan
for the Week

MOUNTAIN MOVING *Faith* FOCUS
FOR THIS WEEK!

....
....
....

THIS WEEK'S GOALS

❯ ....
❯ ....
❯ ....

PRIORITIES

❯ ....
❯ ....
❯ ....
❯ ....

PRAYER CONCERNS

❯ ....
❯ ....
❯ ....
❯ ....

GIVE THANKS FOR

❯ ....
❯ ....
❯ ....
❯ ....

Week in View

Monday	Tuesday	Wednesday

Thursday	Friday	Weekend

Faith verse for the week:

For God so loved the world that He gave His only begotten Son, that whoever believes in Him should not perish but have everlasting life.

John 3:16

Action Plan
for the Week

MOUNTAIN MOVING *Faith* FOCUS
FOR THIS WEEK!

....

....

....

THIS WEEK'S GOALS

◇ ....

◇ ....

◇ ....

PRIORITIES

◇ ....

◇ ....

◇ ....

◇ ....

PRAYER CONCERNS

◇ ....

◇ ....

◇ ....

◇ ....

GIVE THANKS FOR

◇ ....

◇ ....

◇ ....

◇ ....

Week in View

dates: Monday, December 14 to Sunday, December 20

Monday	Tuesday	Wednesday

Thursday	Friday	Weekend

Faith verse for the week:

For God did not send His Son into the world to condemn the world,
but that the world through Him might be saved.
John 3:17

Action Plan
for the Week

MOUNTAIN MOVING *Faith* **FOCUS**
FOR THIS WEEK!

....

....

....

THIS WEEK'S GOALS

>< ....

>< ....

>< ....

PRIORITIES

>< ....

>< ....

>< ....

>< ....

PRAYER CONCERNS

>< ....

>< ....

>< ....

>< ....

GIVE THANKS FOR

>< ....

>< ....

>< ....

>< ....

Week in View

dates: **Monday, December 21** to **Sunday, December 27**

Monday	Tuesday	Wednesday

Thursday	Friday	Weekend

Faith verse for the week:

*Through whom also we have access by faith into this grace in which
we stand, and rejoice in hope of the glory of God.*
Romans 5:2

Action Plan
for the Week

MOUNTAIN MOVING *Faith* FOCUS
FOR THIS WEEK!

....

....

....

THIS WEEK'S GOALS

✐ ....

✐ ....

✐ ....

PRIORITIES

✐ ....

✐ ....

✐ ....

✐ ....

PRAYER CONCERNS

✐ ....

✐ ....

✐ ....

✐ ....

GIVE THANKS FOR

✐ ....

✐ ....

✐ ....

✐ ....

Week in View

dates: **Monday, December 28** to **Thursday, December 31**

Monday	Tuesday	Wednesday

Thursday		

Faith verse for the week:

He has delivered us from the power of darkness and conveyed us into the kingdom of the Son of His love, in whom we have redemption through His blood, the forgiveness of sins.
Colossians 1:13-14

Action Plan
for the Week

MOUNTAIN MOVING *Faith* FOCUS FOR THIS WEEK!

....

....

....

THIS WEEK'S GOALS

- ....
- ....
- ....

PRIORITIES

- ....
- ....
- ....

PRAYER CONCERNS

- ....
- ....
- ....

GIVE THANKS FOR

- ....
- ....
- ....
- ....

MOUNTAIN MOVING Faith

Inspiring Quotes

"The answer to our fears is faith—real, fear-shrinking faith—in the God who loves us and gave himself for us."
— Jani Ortlund

"Faith and prayer are the vitamins of the soul; man cannot live in health without them."
— Mahalia Jackson

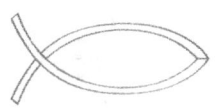

A Glance at 2027

JANUARY

S	M	T	W	T	F	S
					1	2
3	4	5	6	7	8	9
10	11	12	13	14	15	16
17	18	19	20	21	22	23
24	25	26	27	28	29	30
31						

FEBRUARY

S	M	T	W	T	F	S
	1	2	3	4	5	6
7	8	9	10	11	12	13
14	15	16	17	18	19	20
21	22	23	24	25	26	27
28						

MARCH

S	M	T	W	T	F	S
	1	2	3	4	5	6
7	8	9	10	11	12	13
14	15	16	17	18	19	20
21	22	23	24	25	26	27
28	29	30	31			

APRIL

S	M	T	W	T	F	S
				1	2	3
4	5	6	7	8	9	10
11	12	13	14	15	16	17
18	19	20	21	22	23	24
25	26	27	28	29	30	

MAY

S	M	T	W	T	F	S
						1
2	3	4	5	6	7	8
9	10	11	12	13	14	15
16	17	18	19	20	21	22
23	24	25	26	27	28	29
30	31					

JUNE

S	M	T	W	T	F	S
		1	2	3	4	5
6	7	8	9	10	11	12
13	14	15	16	17	18	19
20	21	22	23	24	25	26
27	28	29	30			

JULY

S	M	T	W	T	F	S
				1	2	3
4	5	6	7	8	9	10
11	12	13	14	15	16	17
18	19	20	21	22	23	24
25	26	27	28	29	30	31

AUGUST

S	M	T	W	T	F	S
1	2	3	4	5	6	7
8	9	10	11	12	13	14
15	16	17	18	19	20	21
22	23	24	25	26	27	28
29	30	31				

SEPTEMBER

S	M	T	W	T	F	S
			1	2	3	4
5	6	7	8	9	10	11
12	13	14	15	16	17	18
19	20	21	22	23	24	25
26	27	28	29	30		

OCTOBER

S	M	T	W	T	F	S
					1	2
3	4	5	6	7	8	9
10	11	12	13	14	15	16
17	18	19	20	21	22	23
24	25	26	27	28	29	30
31						

NOVEMBER

S	M	T	W	T	F	S
	1	2	3	4	5	6
7	8	9	10	11	12	13
14	15	16	17	18	19	20
21	22	23	24	25	26	27
28	29	30				

DECEMBER

S	M	T	W	T	F	S
			1	2	3	4
5	6	7	8	9	10	11
12	13	14	15	16	17	18
19	20	21	22	23	24	25
26	27	28	29	30	31	

MOUNTAIN MOVING *Faith* NOTES

MOUNTAIN MOVING *Faith* NOTES

_____
_____
_____
_____
_____
_____
_____
_____
_____
_____
_____
_____
_____
_____
_____
_____
_____
_____
_____
_____
_____
_____

Faith Sees the Unseen, is Obedient, and Does the Impossible

MOUNTAIN MOVING *Faith* NOTES

_____
_____
_____
_____
_____
_____
_____
_____
_____
_____
_____
_____
_____
_____
_____
_____
_____
_____
_____
_____
_____
_____

Faith Sees the Future, Blesses,
and Worships

MOUNTAIN MOVING *Faith* NOTES

_____
_____
_____
_____
_____
_____
_____
_____
_____
_____
_____
_____
_____
_____
_____
_____
_____
_____
_____
_____

Faith Divinely Declares and
Detects Beauty

MOUNTAIN MOVING *Faith* NOTES

_____
_____
_____
_____
_____
_____
_____
_____
_____
_____
_____
_____
_____
_____
_____
_____
_____
_____
_____
_____
_____
_____
_____
_____

Faith Breaks down Walls, Redeems, and Saves

www.ingramcontent.com/pod-product-compliance
Lightning Source LLC
Chambersburg PA
CBHW081533120626
46550CB00009B/2719